Hattie Naylor in collaboration with Sound&Fury

Going Dark

G000149664

Methuen Drama

Published by Methuen Drama 2012

Methuen Drama, an imprint of Bloomsbury Publishing Plc

1 3 5 7 9 10 8 6 4 2

Methuen Drama
Bloomsbury Publishing Plc
50 Bedford Square
London WC1B 3DP
www.methuendrama.com

ISBN 978 1 408 17849 2

A CIP record for this book is available from the British Library

Available in the USA from Bloomsbury Academic & Professional, 175 Fifth
Avenue/3rd Floor, New York, NY 10010. www.BloomsburyAcademicUSA.com

Typeset by Mark Heslington Ltd, Scarborough, North Yorkshire
Printed and bound in Great Britain by CPI Group (UK) Ltd, Croydon, CR0
4YY

·fueL

presents

Sound&Fury's

Going Dark

Written by

Hattie Naylor

in collaboration with

Sound&Fury

·fueL   **covepark**

LOTTERY FUNDED

Supported by

wellcometrust

ROUNDHOUSE

IOP Institute of Physics

JERWOOD **CHARITABLE FOUNDATION**

Science & Technology
Facilities Council

Sound&Fury are **Mark Espiner**, **Dan Jones** and **Tom Espiner**
Directed by: **Mark Espiner** and **Dan Jones**
Co-creator: **Tom Espiner**
Performed by: **John Mackay**
Design: **Aleš Valášek**
Lighting design: **Guy Hoare**
Sound: **Dan Jones**
Projection design: **Dick Straker**
Touring Production Manager: **Ian Moore**
Touring Production Technician: **Sam Evans** (2011)
and **Neil Sowerby** (2012)

Commissioned by Warwick Arts Centre.
Developed as part of Fuel at the Roundhouse and the Jerwood residencies
at Cove Park which are supported by the Jerwood Charitable Foundation.
Funded by Arts Council England, the Wellcome Trust, the Institute of
Physics and the Science and Technology Facilities Council. Supported
by the Linbury Prize for stage design.

THE LINBURY PRIZE FOR STAGE DESIGN is the only competition
of its kind in the UK.

Founded in 1987 by Anya Sainsbury, the Linbury Prize for Stage Design has
helped discover and launch the careers of over 150 talented young stage
designers. It offers an unparalleled opportunity for exposure and success at a
crucial moment in the careers of graduating designers, and the chance to work
with some of the UK's leading directors, with an important theatre, opera or
dance company.

Some of the most important stage designers working today are previous
winners of the Linbury Prize, including Tim Hatley (whose work includes
Rafta, Rafta at the National Theatre and *Spamalot* in the West End and on
Broadway), Anthony Ward (whose credits include *Oliver!* in the West End, *My
Fair Lady* and *Twelfth Night* at the NT) and Vicki Mortimer (who has designed
extensively for the NT including *Burnt by the Sun* and *Hamlet*).

In July 2009, renowned designers Bob Crowley, Katrina Lindsay and Nick
Ormerod selected a shortlist of twenty-five candidates, from which the four
commissioning companies each chose three finalists to work on designs for
a forthcoming production. Aleš Valášek, who trained on the Motley Theatre
Design course, was one of the four individual winners, and was also named
the overall winner of the Linbury Prize 2009.

The Linbury Prize Committee consists of Caro Newling (Chair), Jon Bausor,
Bob Crowley, Sean Crowley, Professor Pamela Howard, Philip Lawford, Vicki
Mortimer, David Pritchard, Anya Sainsbury CBE. The Linbury Prize is sponsored
by the Linbury Trust, one of the Sainsbury Family Charitable Trusts.

The first show **Sound&Fury** made was staged in total darkness. *War Music*, a poem by Christopher Logue, attempted to tell a small part of the story of the Trojan War, in a blacked-out studio theatre. All our work since has explored, to a greater or lesser extent, sense deprivation. We thought that by cutting off one of the branches of perception we might heighten another for our audience and open up a new way of seeing. So perhaps it was inevitable that at some point we would want to tackle the fascinating subject of perception and sight.

The highly regarded neuro-psychologist Professor Richard Gregory came to see **Sound&Fury**'s production of *War Music* and was interested in the way it was visually stimulating, despite the fact that it was performed in total darkness. He was curious as to how the sound in the show had made the pictures. He acted as an early consultant on *Going Dark* and was very encouraging about the connections that could be made between visual perception and trying to grapple with questions about the cosmos. It was a great sadness for us that he died before he could offer his further input on the show.

This piece takes on two very intriguing and troubling questions that we are all prone to ask ourselves at some time or another. How did we get here? And, how can we be sure, if at all, of our existence and ideas of reality?

It has been an interesting journey to find a form to tell a story that embraces those questions and it has involved a large amount of research including fascinating discussions with experts in visual perception, astrophysicists, planetarium presenters and those becoming removed from the common experience of sighted living and learning how to perceive the world without eyes. We are greatly indebted to all those who have helped us.

Research, though, was only a part of it. There was the writing too, which is, in the devised and collaborative context of how we make theatre, a very broad term.

Sound&Fury and **Hattie Naylor** came together for a fantastic week of idea sharing at the wonderful Cove Park artists' retreat in Scotland. It was the beginning of our collaborative relationship that has forged this text, and which continued in rehearsals with valuable input from John Mackay who performed the piece.

Creating the show for the stage – which became something of a conversation between devising around draft texts and shaping what we had developed in Cove Park together – was a challenging process of experimentation with form and storytelling. We set out to make a journey into blindness, to create a sense of standing on the edge of a personal abyss which could in some way reflect our place – our tiny place – in the vast cosmos.

A very early impulse for *Going Dark* was to set a story inside a planetarium. We were attracted to the theatrical and intimate quality these buildings have. In cities around the world, the planetarium offers a view of the night sky that is free of light pollution, giving audiences an opportunity to escape their hectic everyday worlds. A chance to look at the bigger picture for an hour or so allows us to consider some profound questions and engage briefly with the wider universe – its scale and size in relation to us here on Earth. A visit to a planetarium often leads to some kind of self-reflection.

A planetarium is a bit like a secular church: a place to contemplate the profound without having to lean towards a faith. A church, or rather perhaps a public library, providing a civic function as a place of learning and knowledge, education and entertainment. Guided around the night sky by the narrator, the audience is presented with the staggering amount of what we know about the universe, while simultaneously grappling with the limits of our knowledge and the seemingly unfathomable notions of the boundaries and parameters of time and space.

It's the job of astronomers and cosmologists to question our origins and the seemingly unbounded limits of the universe. Many of the astronomers we spoke to when researching this piece said that children always asked the best questions – and they are questions for which we don't really have answers.

The childlike exploring of the cosmos was something we wanted to feature in the play. The daily routines of preparing for and dealing with the day, the meals, the bedtime stories, all provided us with opportunities for Leo and Max to playfully enquire and even theorise about the size and scale of the universe, about birth and matter, how we got here and what we know.

These conversations were never something we could tightly prescribe for a child to act or deliver, so instead we recorded free-flowing conversations with Tom's son Jack at the ages of six and seven, which provided us with an abundance of raw material. With a little editing we could devise and write scenes for Max and Leo around the words captured in these recordings. The result, we hope, is a natural dialogue which brings the universe fleetingly into the domestic environment of a father and son going about their daily chores.

Without wanting to say much more about the piece, and thereby letting you read and discover it fresh, we will leave you with this thought: seeing is really only a part of the picture, and to see properly takes much more than just sight.

Sound&Fury (Mark Espiner, Tom Espiner, Dan Jones)
and **Hattie Naylor**

Bibliography
Eye and Brain by Professor Richard Gregory (Oxford University Press)
Seeing Through Illusions by Professor Richard Gregory (Oxford University Press)
D. H. Ffytche and R. J. Howard, 'The Perceptual Consequences of Visual Loss: "Positive" Pathologies of Vision', *Brain*, 122, 1999, 1247–60
About Face by Jonathan Cole (MIT Press)
The Mind's Eye by Oliver Sacks (Picador)
Touching the Rock by John M. Hull (Vintage)
The British Retinitis Pigmentosa Society, www.rpfightingblindess.org.uk
The Lighter Side of Gravity by Jayant Vishnu Narlikar (Cambridge University Press)
J. D. Barrow and S. P. Bhavsar, 'What the Astronomer's Eye Tells the Astronomer's Brain', *Quart. J. Roy. Astr. Soc.* 28, 1987, 109–28
Cosmic Imagery by John D. Barrow (Bodley Head)
The Artful Universe by John D. Barrow (Oxford University Press)
Stardust by John Gribbin (Penguin)
Exploring the Planetarium by Patrick Moore (Odhams Books)
The New Patterns in the Sky by Julius Staal (McDonald and Woodward)
Cosmos by Carl Sagan (MacDonald/BBC series)
The Cosmic Connection by Carl Sagan (Coronet Books)
Billions and Billions by Carl Sagan (Headline Book Publishing)
The Brightest Stars by Fred Schaf (Wiley)
An Intimate Look at the Night Sky by Chet Raymo (Walker)
Kepler by Angus Armitage (Faber and Faber)
Kepler by John Banville (Minerva)
The Sleepwalkers by Arthur Koestler (Penguin)
The Grand Design by Stephen Hawking and Leonard Mlodinow (Bantam Books)
M. Thurston, 'An Inquiry into the Emotional Impact of Sight Loss and the Counselling Experiences and Needs of Blind and Partially Sighted People', *Counselling and Psychotherapy Research,* 10(1), March 2010, 3–12

Special thanks to: Professor Trevor Ponman, Dr Somak Raychaudhury, Professor Mike Gunn from the Birmingham University Physics and Astronomy Department, West Midlands Arts, Steve Owens and the Glasgow Science Centre, Dr Marek Kukula, the late Professor Richard Gregory, Professor Brian Rogers, Dr Dominic ffytche, Peter Jones, 2009 MAATP students from Central School of Speech and Drama, London Metropolitan University Performing Arts department, Dr Martin Hendry, Tanvir Bush, Retinitis Pigmentosa Association, Martin Welton, Rosie Tooby, Shonagh Manson, Julian Forrester, Alex Tyrell, Anya Sainsbury, Pamela Howard, Philip Lawford, Red Széll, Shaaron Leverment and Ben Brown from Explorer Dome, Andrew Cohen, Ian Galloway, Sam Evans and Ed Collier.

ARTIST BIOGRAPHIES

SOUND&FURY is a collaborative theatre company directed by Mark Espiner, Tom Espiner and Dan Jones. Their artistic interest is in developing the physical and sonic elements of theatre, offering audiences new ways of experiencing performance and stories in an immersive environment by heightening the aural sense. To achieve these aims, Sound&Fury has, in the past, boldly immersed its audience in total darkness. This unique theatrical device combined with sophisticated surround sound design, imaginative acoustic devices, voice and subtle lighting effects, creates a powerful new language for theatre that has gained the attention of the media and the critics. Previous work includes *The Watery Part of the World* – where the audience was plunged into total darkness to witness the thrill of a nineteenth-century whale hunt – and *Ether Frolics,* which took the audience on a theatrical anaesthetic trip, and the critically acclaimed *Kursk* where Sound&Fury placed its audience in the secret world of a Royal Navy submarine. In each of these cases, fractured images, glimpses of scenes, visual and sonic tricks and a 360-degree soundscape created worlds which redefined the performance space. Audiences have found these experiences thrilling, transporting and disorienting. www.soundandfury.org.uk

DAN JONES has developed a career bringing together music, sound and drama as director, composer and sound designer. He read music at Oxford and studied composition at the Centro Ricerche Musicali, Rome. He recently received BAFTA and Ivor Novello Awards for his score for *Any Human Heart*. Other music includes scores for the Oscar-nominated films *The Tonto Woman* and *Shadow of the Vampire* as well as *David Attenborough's The Life of Mammals.* Orchestral arrangements include work for Alpha, Jarvis Cocker and Massive Attack and music and sound for theatre includes commissions for the RSC, National Theatre, the Donmar and Almeida, including *The City Madam, Through a Glass Darkly* and *The Kitchen* (National Theatre), *Ivan and the Dogs* (Soho) which received an Olivier nomination, and Tim Crouch's award-winning *England*. His sound installations include *Music for Seven Ice Cream Vans* co-commissioned by LIFT and the Sydney Festival, and *Sky Orchestra* (with Luke Jerram) which creates a giant surround-sound music system over cities touring internationally and launching the Sydney Festival 2007. As a theatre director he trained at the Banff Centre for the Arts and co-founded Sound&Fury, for whom he has co-directed and sound designed *War Music, Ether*

Frolics, *Kursk* and *Going Dark*. *Kursk* won a special Jury prize for sound design at the 2011 Prague Quadrennial.

MARK ESPINER is a theatre director and freelance writer. He has contributed to *The Sunday Times*, *Independent*, BBC Radio 3, the *Guardian* and the *Financial Times* on music and the arts. As co-artistic director of Sound&Fury, the theatre company he co-founded with Dan Jones and Tom Espiner, he has directed Christopher Logue's *War Music* and *The Watery Part of the World*, a piece based on Herman Melville's *Moby Dick*; *Ether Frolics* – made in collaboration with artists from the Shunt Collective (Shunt Vaults and Edinburgh Fringe); *Names of the Dead*, a staged musical war memorial to the dead of the Iraq war, created collaboratively with artist Mark Anstee, composer Stephen McNeff and the Duke Quartet (BAC); *Kursk* (both 2009; 2010 UK tour and Sydney Opera House 2011) and *Going Dark* (2011 and 2012 tours). He lives in Berlin.

TOM ESPINER trained at Bristol Old Vic Theatre School and is a co-founder of Sound&Fury, with whom he has co-written, co-devised and performed in *Ether Frolics* (Shunt Vaults), *The Watery Part of the World* and *War Music* (BAC, This Way Up Tour), and Sound&Fury's *Kursk* (Young Vic, Edinburgh 2009, 2010 UK tour, Sydney Opera House 2011). He also co-devised *Going Dark* (2011 and 2012 tours). Other theatre includes: *Peggy for You* (Hampstead, West End, tour), *The Winter's Tale, Twelfth Night, Macbeth* (Shakespeare at the Tobacco Factory, Barbican Pit), *Anything Goes* and *Love's Labour's Lost* (NT), *Jason and the Argonauts* (BAC), *The Firework Maker's Daughter* (Told By An Idiot/Lyric Hammersmith), Bryony Lavery's *Yikes!* (Unicorn) and *Bloody Chamber* (Northern Stage). Television and film: *Anybody's Nightmare, The Bill, Without Motive, Ancient Rome* (BBC) and *Stoned* (Scala Films). Tom has also worked as a Foley artist for BBC Nature documentaries and other TV and film productions.

HATTIE NAYLOR was studying painting at the Slade School of Art when her first play was accepted in the BBC Radio Young Playwrights Festival. She has won several national and international awards for her plays and has had over thirty plays, three short stories and an opera broadcast on BBC Radio 4 and/or 3. *Ivan and the Dogs* for Soho Theatre with ATC was nominated in the 2010 Olivier Awards for Outstanding Achievement. The radio version of *Ivan and the Dogs*, directed and edited by Paul Dodgson, won the Tinniswood Award for Best Original Radio Drama in 2009.

Other recent theatre productions include a stage version of *Ben Hur* for a cast of 180, a bloodthirsty reworking of *The Nutcracker* for Theatre Royal Bath, and the opera *Piccard in Space* with composer Will Gregory (Goldfrapp) for Radio 3 and the Southbank, conducted by Charles Hazlewood, directed by Jude Kelly. Other recent work includes *The Diaries of Samuel Pepys*, and *Sleeping Beauty and the Dark Art of Forgetting*, both for Radio 4.

JOHN MACKAY Previous work for Sound&Fury: *War Music* and *The Watery Part of the World* (BAC, This Way Up Tour). Other theatre work includes: *Antony and Cleopatra, Little Eagles, The Grain Store, The Histories, Twelfth Night, Pilate, Hamlet, As You Like It, Macbeth* (RSC), *Julius Caesar, The Winter's Tale, King Lear* (RSC and Lincoln Center Festival, New York); *Six Characters in Search of an Author* (Headlong); *Dark Earth* (Traverse); *All My Sons* (York Theatre Royal); *Troilus and Cressida, As You Like It, The Winter's Tale* and *Measure for Measure* (Shakespeare at the Tobacco Factory) and *The Accidental Death of a Maniac* (Hysterick Theatre Tokyo). Work in television includes *Law and Order, Casualty, Trial and Retribution*, and *Doc Martin*. Radio includes: *Heart of Darkness, Night and Day, Madeleine, Soldier Soldier* and *The Illiad* (BBC Radio).

ALEŠ VALÁŠEK was born in the Czech Republic. In 2009 Aleš became the overall winner of the prestigious Linbury Prize for Stage Design for the design for *Going Dark*.

Aleš graduated from the Motley Theatre Design Course directed by Alison Chitty in 2008. Before going to Motley, Aleš studied Costume Design at the Academy of Performing Arts in Prague under Professor Jana Zbořilová. While studying, Aleš designed costumes for productions including *Like Totally Weird, The Flying Dutchman,* and *West Side Story*. In 2004, he was appointed Assistant Costume Designer and Costume Supervisor for the Czech premiere of *Miss Saigon*. In 2006 while at London College of Fashion, Aleš assisted costume designer Sue Willmington on *Show Boat* (Royal Albert Hall) and assisted Peter Davison on the world premiere of the musical *Rebecca* (Raimund Theatre, Vienna). After Motley, Aleš designed *My Feet May Take a Little While* (Arcola Theatre) and *Mary Postgate* (Edinburgh Festival).

In 2010 Aleš became the second designer in the world to design an original concept for the new version of the musical *Marguerite* by Michel Legrand and the creators of *Les Misérables,* Alain Boublil and Claude-Michel Schönberg, in collaboration with Marie Zamora and John Dempsey. His recent design work includes costume design for Rubinstein's opera *Demon*, set and costume design for *The Little Shop of Horrors* (Městské divadlo Brno, Brno, Czech Republic) and set design for the Czech premiere of the Broadway musical *Curtains* (Hudební divadlo Karlín, Czech Republic). Alongside that Aleš designed costumes for Gluck's *Orfeo ed Euridice*. Aleš was nominated by the audience for Wings Theatre Award 'Best Artistic Achievement of the Season' category for *The Little Shop of Horrors*.

GUY HOARE Theatre includes: *Peter Pan* (National Theatre of Scotland); *Be Near Me; Serenading Louie* (Donmar); *A Delicate Balance; Waste* (Almeida); *Othello* (West End); *Electra* (The Gate); *Faith Healer* (Bristol Old Vic); *A Christmas Carol; The Lion, the Witch and the Wardrobe* (Birmingham Rep); *In Basildon* (Royal Court); *And No More Shall We Part* (Hampstead).

Dance includes: *The Metamorphosis* (ROH2/Arthur Pita); *Mischief* (Theatre Rites); *The Land of Yes, The Land of No* (Sydney Dance Company); *Frontline* (Aterbaletto); *Square Map of Q4* (Bonachela Dance Company); *And Who Shall Come to the Ball?* (Candoco*); Love and War; Sea of Bones*; *Bad History; Green Apples; Dive* (Mark Bruce Company); *Havana Rakatan* (Sadler's Wells); *Pavlova's Dogs* (Scottish Dance Theatre).

Opera includes: *The Cunning Little Vixen* (National Theatre Brno); *La Clemenza di Tito; Gianni Schicchi; Il Tabarro; Fantastic Mr Fox; Promised End; The Duenna; The Magic Flute; Katya Kabanova; Don Giovanni; Anna Bolena; Susannah; The Seraglio; Eugene Onegin* (English Touring Opera).

Musicals include: *The Witches of Eastwick; All the Fun of the Fair; Aspects of Love* (UK tours); *Annie* (West Yorkshire Playhouse).

DICK STRAKER is a video and projection designer and provides image production services for theatre, performance and visual arts through his company Mesmer.

Recent designs have included *Orpheus and Eurydice* (NYT Waterloo Tunnels), *Tristan and Isolde* (Grange Park Opera), *Tiger Country* (Hampstead Theatre), *The King and I* (Curve Theatre, Leicester), *Desire Under the Elms* (The New Vic, Newcastle Under Lyme), *Seize the Day* (The Tricycle), *The Tales of Ballycumber* (The Abbey, Dublin), *The Mountaintop* (Trafalgar Studios), which won an Olivier Award for best new play and *Just Add Water* for Shobana Jeyasingh Dance Company (The Linbury).

DR DOMINIC FFYTCHE is a Clinical Senior Lecturer at the Institute of Psychiatry, King's College London. He developed a research interest into visual perception and its disorders while a Wellcome Trust Vision Fellow and his early work on the Charles Bonnet Syndrome formed part of his Wellcome Trust Clinician Scientist Fellowship. He has written extensively on neuroscientific, clinical and philosophical aspects of the Charles Bonnet Syndrome, with his research in this area published in high-impact journals such as *Nature Neuroscience*. He advises the Macular Disease Society and Royal National Institute for the Blind on issues related to the Charles Bonnet Syndrome. He has acted as consultant and appeared in a number of television and radio programmes featuring the Charles Bonnet Syndrome.

Sound&Fury are produced by **Fuel**. Fuel produce fresh work for adventurous people by inspiring artists. Founded in 2004 and led by Louise Blackwell and Kate McGrath, Fuel is a producing organisation working in partnership with some of the most exciting theatre artists in the UK to develop, create and present new work for all.

Fuel is currently producing projects with Will Adamsdale, Belarus Free Theatre, Clod Ensemble, Inua Ellams, Fevered Sleep, David Rosenberg, Sound&Fury, Uninvited Guests and Melanie Wilson. Fuel runs a rolling internship scheme. Our current producing intern is Hannah Myers from Central School of Speech and Drama. For further information on Fuel, our artists, our team and our internships, please visit *www.fueltheatre.com* or call 020 7228 6688.

Fuel's recent projects include: *The Simple Things in Life* (Edinburgh Fringe, Latitude, Big Chill 2011); *Minsk 2011* (Belarus Free Theatre, Edinburgh 2011); *Jackson's Way: The London Jacksathon!* (Will Adamsdale); *Electric Hotel* (Requardt & Rosenberg); *Kursk* (Sound&Fury); *MUST: The Inside Story* (Peggy Shaw and Clod Ensemble); *Love Letters Straight from Your Heart* (Uninvited Guests); *The Forest* and *On Ageing* (Fevered Sleep); *The 14th Tale* and *Untitled* (Inua Ellams); *An Anatomie in Four Quarters* (Clod Ensemble) and *Autobiographer* (Melanie Wilson).

'One of the most exciting and indispensable producing outfits working in British theatre today.' Guardian

'The maverick producing organisation who are prepared to invest in adventurous artists.' The Herald

Directors	**Kate McGrath** & **Louise Blackwell**
Executive Director	**Ed Errington**
Producer	**Christina Elliot**
Head of Production	**Stuart Heyes**
Project Managers	**Alice Massey** & **Rosalind Wynn**
Deputy Production Manager	**Ian Moore**
Administrator	**Natalie Dibsdale**

MAKE YOUR MARK ON SOUND&FURY AND FUEL

At Fuel we work with artists and theatre companies like Sound&Fury to create new experiences for you to enjoy. We believe in these aims and work hard every day to make them happen.

If you would like to help us, visit our website at fueltheatre.com and click on 'support'. There are lots of ways you can get involved. Just £5 a month will help make our ambitions real. In return we'll give you exclusive benefits and the inside story on what we're up to. You'll make great ideas come to life for the broadest possible audience.

If you would like to find out more about supporting Sound&Fury specifically please email info@fueltheatre.com. We can tailor a package which allows you to support Sound&Fury to create new work, like *Going Dark*, and to follow their progress each step of the way.

You'll keep us going.

Thank you from all of us.

A big thank you to Fuel's current supporters

Fuel is an Arts Council England regularly funded organisation

WITH THANKS TO OUR CATALYSTS:
Sean Egan, James Mackenzie-Blackman, Michael Morris, Sarah Preece, Sarah Quelch, John Tiffany and Nick Williams

2012 TOUR DATES:

DRUM THEATRE, PLYMOUTH
8–11 February
theatreroyal.com | 01752 267 222

ABERYSTWYTH ARTS CENTRE
13–17 February
aber.ac.uk/artscentre | 01970 62 32 32

WALES MILLENNIUM CENTRE
21 & 22 February
wmc.org.uk | 029 2063 6464

UNITY THEATRE, LIVERPOOL
24 & 25 February
unitytheatreliverpool.co.uk | 0844 873 2888

HULL TRUCK THEATRE
28 & 29 February
hulltruck.co.uk | 01482 323 638

LAKESIDE THEATRE, COLCHESTER
3 March
essex.ac.uk/artson5 | 01206 873 288/573 948

YOUNG VIC, LONDON
6–24 March
youngvic.org | 020 7922 2922

Going Dark

Characters

Max

(Recorded voices)
Leo
Voiceover Artist
Optician

1. Nature and the Universe

Spring bird song, breathing, a gentle evening wind stirs grass at our feet, and then birch trees slightly further away. The bird song fades and beyond, in a valley of trees, an owl, distant thunder ripples across the sky. And then light rain, drop by drop, falls on leaves of the trees and then the grass around us. Silence.

2. Shaving and Robots

Max *is shaving.* **Leo** *is talking to him while playing with his toys and moving around the house.*

Leo   We don't know where we're from . . . We got found . . . I made . . . My partner the leader, I am the main leader /

Max (*imitating* **Leo** *doing robot voices and then resumes his own voice*)   What are you doing?

Leo   I am making a rocket that can go through the Sun.

Max   The Sun?

Leo   Right through the Sun.

Max   Right through the Sun? That's going to be pretty hot . . . So once you've gone through the Sun, where else are you going to go to?

Leo   Sun.

Max   Yeah.

Leo   Jupiter.

Max   Jupiter, OK.

Leo   The universe . . .

Max   The universe – that's pretty big. How big's the universe, Leo?

Leo   Well that's impossible to know . . .

And also they can't measure it with a rocket because they don't have a measuring tape on a rocket.

Max (*laughs*)   You'd need a pretty big measuring tape too! So Leo where else would you want to go?

Leo   Well I would go . . . to the other side.

Max   Um – hmm – yeah?

Leo   Do you know where I'd go to the other side of?

Max   Where would you go to the other side of?

Leo   I would go to a different galaxy.

Max   A different galaxy? Which galaxy?

Leo   The Milky Way.

Max   The Milky Way? But that's the galaxy we're already in, isn't it?

Leo   The non-star Milky Way!!

Max   The non-star Milky Way – a galaxy without stars. That would be a dark place Leo . . .

Leo   What's the bit before space?

Max   Er – what, what do you mean? Er . . . you mean the Big Bang?

Leo   Um, no /

Max   What – the bit before we get to space?

Leo   Yes.

Max   You mean the atmosphere?

Leo   Yes, the atmosphere.

Max   Well, that's a bit complicated – the atmosphere. The atmosphere – there's clouds and there's sky /

Leo   The reason why /

Max   Oh /

Leo   – there is clouds – ouds – ouds /

Max (*encouraging him to go on*)   Yes . . .

Leo   is 'cause . . .

Max   Yes.

Leo   I think . . .

Max   Yeah.

Leo   The bit before space . . .

Max   Yeah go on –

Leo   clunges up like /

Max   Clunges up yeah.

Leo   squadgy things with water.

Max   Squadgy things with water – yeah /

Leo   And it smashes into tiny bits . . . and that creates rain . . . and snow.

And it's like the clouds doing a wee.

Max   Well we don't have to worry about that tonight, the weather man says it was going to be clear tonight and there's no moon so the sky should be pitch black.

Leo   It's not black it's very very very very dark blue.

Max   OK it's very very very very very very very very very very very very very very very very very dark blue.

Leo   Yeah – not that blue, but quite blue.

Max   OK, well quite blue.

Leo   Do you know how I know that? Because I watch films . . . with that and also I've been looking up.

Max   Alright smartipants. Look, we're going to be late for dinner. Grandad's got his new telescope . . . So come on. Chop chop! Where are your shoes!? Put your shoes on!

Leo (*clears his throat*)   The reason why wind makes is probably because ALL space moves with big jolt . . . (*etc. etc.*)

Leo's *voice fades as he walks off talking about the weather /*
atmosphere /.

Max (*calling out to him*)   LEO! GET YOUR SHOES!

Max *catches himself in the mirror; he notices something in his*
peripheral vision is not quite right. He tests his visual field. Looks in
the mirror out of the edge of his eye.

Leo   What is the furthest thing?

WHAT IS THE FURTHEST THING?

Continuous to next scene . . .

3. Planetarium 1: How far can you see?

Max   What is the furthest thing?

How far do you think you can see?

As far as the horizon? From the top of the London Eye . . .
Basildon, maybe?

The Sun? That's around 93 million miles away.

You might think you can't see very far at night, but when the Earth turns us away from the dazzling light of the Sun, we have a chance to peer into the universe.

Night reveals what the bright day hides.

So let's have a look.

He turns on the projector.

All the stars you can see in the sky are part of our galaxy, the Milky Way. That's what we are part of and what you can see. Only our galaxy.

Until only ninety years ago we thought that this – the view of our night sky from Earth – was the whole universe. That's what we thought.

But then, in 1923, the astronomer Edwin Hubble took a photo through his telescope of a dim smudge of light in the night sky. He thought it was a nebula – a cloud of gas. But when he looked closely at it he saw tiny pinpricks of light, each one a star. It was as if there was a whole new universe outside our own. It was, in fact, another galaxy. The Andromeda Galaxy. And in that moment our notion of the cosmos suddenly exploded.

But Andromeda is just the tip of a colossal galactic iceberg; we are surrounded by something like 500 billion galaxies – each containing hundreds of billions of stars. Andromeda is just the nearest one to us.

How far can you see?

Andromeda is the furthest thing you can see with the naked eye.

That means you can see 2.5 million light years away.

Just so we're clear, one light year is 5,865 billion, 696 million miles.

So Andromeda is 2.5 million times that – that's how far you can see.

(*ad lib*) Pretty impressive, huh?

So – let's find this furthest thing we can see with the naked eye. This Andromeda.

First find Polaris, the pole star. Polaris is fixed, it doesn't move, so it's a great guiding star to help you find your way around the night sky and it lies directly between the Plough and this bright uneven W (or M) we call Cassiopeia.

The right half of the Cassiopeia W points like an arrow to Andromeda. But how far from Cassiopeia is it?

Do you see Pegasus? The main part of Pegasus is a big empty rectangle. Andromeda lies halfway between that rectangle and Cassiopeia. Just here.

Andromeda is elusive if you look at her directly – you'll need to use your peripheral vision. She is faint but if you look out of the corner of your eye, you'll see her.

Just look to the side.

She is the only galaxy we can see with the naked eye . . .

And she is our mirror. From her our galaxy, the Milky Way, would look just like that little smudge looks to us in the night sky.

4. The Eye Test

Optician   OK Max, are you comfortable?

Max   Yes

Optician   Keep your eye on the white dot at the centre of the screen.

I need you to keep focused on that white dot . . .

Now, you'll see flashes, red dots, appearing on lots of different places on the screen. Randomly. I want you to click every time you can see a red flash. We're testing for your peripheral vision.

OK let's start. Keep your eye on the dot in front of you –

A sequence of red dots start to appear, at first in the area immediately ahead of **Max** *(NB to LX: One of the forward lights is not used yet**).* **Max** *sees all of these and correspondingly a bleep is heard following each red dot – a regular reassuring rhythm.*

The rhythm is broken after about eight bleeps as we see one of the lights to the far side of his field of view not triggering a response. Perhaps this is normal – we're not sure. Other more forward intervening dots still triggering the bleeps. This continues for another eight or nine bleeps – a less regular rhythm.

Then another dot (**) quite far forward also fails to trigger a bleep. Is it worse than we thought? The doctor tries another dot quite far forward – fine, no problem – but returns to the problem dot. Again no response. And yet again. Nothing. The rhythm has broken down completely.

Optician I just need to check you're keeping your focus on the central white dot.

Max Yes.

Optician OK, let's try that again.

The red lights appear again as the test recommences. The silence speaks volumes as to how much of his peripheral vision has disappeared. The bleeps cross fade into the following scene.

(Technical note: the dots appear for three seconds each with a three-second pause between – i.e. the dots cycle over six seconds).

5. Planetarium 2: The Story of Dhruv

Max All cultures have looked up at the night sky, and seen patterns in the stars and told stories about them.

Look at these seven bright ones here.

We call them the Plough, Americans call it the Big Dipper, the French call it *le casserole*.

Whatever you call it, if you take the two stars on this outer edge, join them up and carry on in a straight line, you come to a dim star. Polaris. The pole star.

It sits directly above the north pole, so as the earth spins Polaris appears to stay still while all the others move.

The stars rotate around the pole star above.

It's the only star that does so, and for that reason it's been used by sailors and travellers as a reliable guiding star.

In India, they call Polaris Dhruv Tara and this is their story as to why the star never moves . . .

SFX: Indian music.

Dhruv was the son of King Uttanapada; but the King took a second wife and had another son and favoured him, not Dhruv.

One day Dhruv climbed on to his father's lap but the King's second wife threw him off, warning Dhruv he had no right to sit there.

Dhruv, confused and hurt, ran to his mother and stayed by her all day, silent and sad. He asked her if there was anyone more powerful than his father the King. 'Yes,' she said, 'the great God Vishnu who lives in the mountains.'

That night Dhruv decided to walk to the mountains. He climbed to the very top, and came to the edge of the Northern Sky.

There, Dhruv stopped and meditated, thinking only of Vishnu. His meditations were so intense that many sages and gods gathered round him to watch. They had never seen one so still, so they tested him with demons and snakes to distract him – but nothing could disturb Dhruv.

Finally the great Vishnu himself was drawn by the full courage and constancy of the little boy's meditations; he appeared to the child and offered him anything he wished.

Continuous to . . .

6. The Bedtime Story of Dhruv

Max (*making a mobile to hang over* **Leo**'s *bed*)   . . . Anything Leo, imagine that.

Leo   Yeah.

Max   But Dhruv remained completely silent and still, for what seemed like years – he thought of Vishnu for that long. Finally the great god came down from above and picked up little Dhruv and took him up, up high into the night sky. And he transformed him into . . .?

Leo   Stars probably –

Max   Well not just stars but a very special star for a special boy. Do you know where this star is?

Leo   Right in the centre of the universe!

Max   Well in a way yes. He was turned into the pole star. And he still shines up there twinkling for all children who are feeling lost and longing for fairness in the world. And do you remember the sages who had watched Dhruv as he prayed, Leo?

Leo   Yes.

Max   Well Vishnu turned them into seven bright stars. And Indian children call them Saptarish – we call it the Plough – and they move around little Dhruv, the pole star, guarding him still.

OK. Time for bed. Shall we switch the lights off?

Leo   Yeah.

Max   Sleep tight.

Lights out.

7. The Dark Room: A Memory

In red light **Max** *pours chemicals gingerly into a tray. He lowers a sheet of photographic paper in and, setting a timer, watches a black-and-white house image magically appear.*

He removes the photo of the house from the tray, lifting and examining it, as it slowly and magically comes to life with sound and colour.

Blackout.

8. Total Darkness: Sound of the Street

Total darkness. Sound.

We leave the Planetarium into a maniacally busy street with relentless traffic. It is rush hour and raining heavily. People's voices brush in and out of earshot, swiping past us, as they hurry for shelter. We approach the sound of a pelican crossing, its bleeps getting closer. All the while **Max***'s white stick is tapping its way through this melee, barely heard. The traffic gets louder as we approach and the pelican stops bleeping and as if a dam has burst a surge of traffic collectively opens throttles surging past and away into a rumble. An angry horn dopplers past as if* **Max** *may have misjudged the edge of the pavement.*

Fade.

9. The Helpline

Max *is carrying an envelope. He sits down at home and opens it. We can hear* **Leo** *playing in the background/watching TV. He reads the letter which is consolidating the diagnosis he has just had from his consultant. There are some other brochures of the 'Living with Blindness' kind and 'What is RP?'. He sits back trying to absorb the lead weight which has just landed on his desk. He picks up the letter again and then grabs his phone and dials a number for the RP Helpline written down on the letter.*

Hi.

My doctor gave me this number. There are a few things I wanted to ask about . . .

No, no. No, I'm the first I know of in my family to have it.

Well my doctor said it could be fast. Can you give me an idea of what I can expect? . . .

Oh I see.

Right.

No that's fine I will go back to him for that . . .

Sure, OK. Well. The thing I'm worried about, the thing I'm most worried about is – that if my sight deteriorates quickly – I've got a little boy . . .

He's six.

Leo.

(*laughs*) Yes.

Well, what I've started to do is . . . I've tried to put things so I know where they are, where I can find them easily . . . He has a tendency to move things and leave things lying around . . .

Actually, I'm a single parent.

Er . . . He gets on very well with my parents, but I can manage.

Are you saying that I can't . . . that I won't be able to look after him on my own with this?

Really? Social Services? Surely . . .

We're close. We do a lot of stuff – well everything – together. I drive him to things, used to drive him to things, clearly I can't do that now . . .

I don't want to go down that route. Look, my relationship with my son is based on me being with him, and looking after him. Being his dad. I mean, surely he and I can both adapt to this without interference – and work things out together /

/ Of course. I don't want to burden him with anything.

Like what?

Well, surely, I'm not going to forget what he looks like.

Yeah, OK, so . . .

Really?

No that's OK.

Look, I need to go now, I think my son needs me.

No, no you've been a great help.

I will. Thanks.

OK, thanks.

Bye.

10. Planetarium 3: Stardust

Max   On a clear night, without the glare of city lights, you will probably be able to see between two and three thousand stars. It will look something like this.

But what are the stars? Where did they come from? And besides twinkling beautifully, what do they mean to us?

There is one star that means a huge amount to us; it's the one nearest to us and without it we wouldn't exist. It is, of course, the Sun.

The Sun provides our planet with heat and light and it will go on doing so steadily for the next four billion years or so. We are just the right distance from it for life to thrive on Earth.

All these stars are other suns. They may look small from here but they are in fact gigantic balls of gas.

So how are they made?

Hydrogen gas – the simplest and lightest gas of all – can be found all over the universe, often in great clouds. When part of a cloud cools and shrinks, under the pull of its own gravity a dense centre forms. More and more hydrogen is drawn in – putting more and more pressure on this centre; the hydrogen is packed tighter and tighter together and the temperature spirals.

At a critical point, with enough heat and pressure, the hydrogen atoms start fusing together and the star bursts into life – a vast nuclear reaction releasing great heat and light.

This fusion of hydrogen creates an entirely new element, helium. All these stars are doing pretty much what the Sun is doing: converting hydrogen into helium.

But what happens when the hydrogen runs out?

This is the constellation of Orion. There's Orion's belt – this is Betelgeuse – the 'armpit' of Orion. Betelgeuse is a red supergiant five hundred times the size of our Sun. After it has turned all its hydrogen into helium, Betelgeuse will carry on crushing and fusing atoms, converting the helium into carbon. As the star becomes older and denser it will convert the carbon atoms into oxygen and will carry on fusing more and more complex elements until the star begins to collapse, overwhelmed by its own gravity. The final collapse triggers a sudden cataclysmic explosion – a supernova.

If you looked through a telescope at this part of the sky in the constellation of Taurus the bull you would see a fuzzy cloud known as the Crab Nebula. This is the debris from a supernova explosion which occurred a thousand years ago.

The people who saw it in 1054 AD said it was so bright that it was visible during the day – and that you could even read by its light at night.

The death of stars such as these seeds the universe with the elements. When stars explode they scatter carbon, oxygen, and all the other things they have made across space. These scattered elements are the building blocks for life: the carbon in every living thing on Earth, the oxygen in your lungs, the calcium in your bones, the traces of iron in your blood, all come from these giant creative furnaces that we call stars.

So what do the stars mean to us? They mean everything.

We are literally made from scattered stardust. What started off as a big ball of hydrogen has ended up as you.

The big question is – where did all this hydrogen come from in the first place?

11. Kitchen Conversation

Max *is in the kitchen, trying to prepare* **Leo***'s supper.*

Leo   The question is . . .

Max   Er . . . The question is how many sausages do you want?

Leo   We . . .

Max   Yeah?

Leo   . . . are material.

Max   Yes, I know . . .

Leo   Everything in the . . . The universe is a material.

Max   Uh huh?

Leo   . . . and everything in it is a material.

Max   Yeah . . .

Leo   The question is . . .

Max   The question is what?

Leo   Everything on Earth is a material . . .

Max   That's very good Leo. And where did the material come from? How was this material made?

Leo   No one made it. It just made itself. That's what material does. Then animals started coming with their material . . .

Max   Well – Leo how do you think the material made itself before all the animals?

Leo (*starting to go off*)   THAT'S THE QUESTION WE DON'T KNOW – EVEN SCIENTISTS DON'T KNOW.

Max   Well actually –

Leo (*still off*)   Well I'll show, well well well well . . . what we're sitting on is material . . . We are material so don't forget . . . only – not only . . .

Max (*calling*)   Leo?

Leo   . . . Squishy stuff is material.

Max   Leo? Come back – I need to talk to you.

Leo (*off*)   Yes. (*Brains.*) 'DETONATION IN FOUR SECONDS!'

Max   Leo – Leave the Thunderbirds alone and come in here for a minute. Was that Brains?

Leo (*returning*)   Yeah.

Max   Leo.

He waits for **Leo** *to come into the room.*

Leo   Can I do a tiny bit more statements?

Max   Not just yet. Leo – you know Daddy stopped driving the car? . . .

Leo   Yes . . .

Max   And – he's also been bumping into things?

Leo   Yeah . . .

Max   Yeah – why do you think that is?

Leo   Don't know . . .

Max   Do you want to know why?

Leo   'MR TRACY – I HAVE AN IDEA!'

Pause.

Max   OK . . . Do you want to know why, Leo . . . /

Leo   'YOU'RE RUNNING LOW ON FUEL!'

Max   OK, time to refuel! – Thunderbirds are go! Let's get you some more sausages!

Blackout.

12. Planetarium 4: The Big Bang

So the question is where did all the hydrogen, which made all these stars, come from?

Going back about 300,000 years before the very first stars were even born, we believe that all this hydrogen and space itself was packed into a tiny, tiny speck of incredible density.

And from this speck at the beginning of time – yes, there was no time before that moment – the universe explodes into existence.

We call this the Big Bang. In three minutes the universe was a hundred billion miles across. And all the hydrogen in the universe – that includes the hydrogen atoms in every drop of water on Earth – was made in that first explosion 13.7 billion years ago. Think of that every time you run a bath . . . every time you have a glass of water. You're drinking Big Bang! Can I have a glass of Big Bang please? Thank you very much.

So here we are – gazing at these two or three thousand stars up above us and they all look very beautiful – some with quite exotic-sounding names like Betelgeuse, Aldebaran and Zubeneschamali. And we think: 'How amazing I come from a star! I'm literally made from stardust . . .'

But are you struggling with the idea that all of this – everything we know and experience – everything we feel and imagine! – started from a tiny speck? That there is no 'before' before the Big Bang?

13. Talking to the Parents

Max *is at home. He gets a pair of RP simulation glasses out of a packet (sent to him from the British Retinitis Pigmentosa Association) and tries them on. He walks awkwardly about the space. He goes back to the pamphlet that came with them and reads, and is clearly unhappy with the information.*

Mobile phone rings.

Max Hi Dad.

Good. Yes. Good.

Fine. He's fine. He's teaching me things now. He can find Sirius all by himself.

Well, I think he sort of knows; he can join the dots, Dad. I've told him I've got to give up the car, he's seen me bumping into things and I trod on his favourite rocket yesterday which didn't make me feel too great.

No.

Because that's something we do together and it's important I do that with him.

No, no, no, please, Dad no, no, no . . .

Hi Mum.

Mum . . .

Mum. Mum. It's alright. I'll be alright. Don't cry.

Leo will be fine.

I don't want to burden him yet. Six-year-olds can work out lots of things for themselves, they don't need to be told everything . . .

I am. I am. I'm OK right now!

I don't want to do that.

(*Angrily.*) Jesus Mum! I'm trying to take it all in myself at the moment.

Mum?

Is she alright, Dad?

We're trying to find a solution at work. They're going to try me recording my presentations which they'll put together with visuals. And they'll get me in to do Q&A sessions.

Yes. They'll have a Q&A with me after each presentation.

Dad, I told Mum, I don't want to do that.

No, I can cope. I don't stop being his dad just 'cause of this. We'll manage together. We both need to adapt . . .

Look, you're my dad not his. And I'm not your child. I don't need that kind of help.

Dad, thanks. But no. Why do you think you have to do that?

Look, I've got to go. I'll call you.

14. Max at Leo's Bedside

I was six, your age and Granny and Grandad were about to move, and I loved our old house – it had a huge garden at the back and a view with a wood and hills and then mountains at the back, but Grandad had just got a new job and we had to move to the town. So this was like our goodbye to the garden. And we'd just finished tea and Grandad took me outside and he held my hand and we just looked. And there were birds. And it's evening.

Into FX of opening scene.

And there are trees and they are white like silver, birch trees, and the grass moves, and the leaves move on the trees. And further off I can see the wood, and I can hear a barn owl. Then Leo, then there's thunder, and we watch together the mountains, illuminated, as the Sun goes down, in great sudden flashes.

And then it begins to rain. First one drop and then another and another. But we just stand in the rain, we stand in the rain my father and me. It is the most fantastic picture, Leo, my father and me.

He looks at **Leo**. *Pause.*

Leo   Daddy.

Max   Yes.

Leo   Why are you staring at me?

15. Planetarium 5: Newton and Colour

Hello everyone and welcome. My name's Max and I'm your guide to the night sky today. I'm going to dim the lights straight away because I'd like to show you something.

In 1671 Isaac Newton took one of these – it's a glass prism – and he held it up to a beam of sunlight.

This is what happened:

Newton realised that white sunlight was made up of all these colours. But this visible spectrum or rainbow is just one part of a much wider spectrum of invisible waves.

The invisible spectrum extends past the colour red to infra-red, and on further to microwaves and then radio waves. In the other direction, past blue we find ultraviolet, and then ever smaller waves: x-rays and gamma rays.

So why do we only see this part? It's as if we're only hearing a few notes on a piano keyboard when there's so much more. Our eyes are attuned to these wavelengths because these are the ones that our local star produces in abundance. Our eyes have sensibly evolved to exploit what's most available.

We experience these different wavelengths as different colours, but it's the brain that *creates* the sensation of colour – and sometimes it makes revealing mistakes . . .

Look at this picture. Look at the two crosses. They look as if they are different colours, don't they? But they are, in fact, *exactly* the same.

If you want proof – look here, where the two crosses join.

What you think you see is what your brain has created for you from the light that pours into each pupil. The brain works furiously to make sense of all this incoming information and magically distils it into the splendour of sight.

Seeing feels passive, effortless – but in reality, behind the scenes, your brain is turning somersaults.

One part of the brain deals with rotation, another with straight edges, another with form, another with colour. And all of those inputs seamlessly combine to create a *representation* of the world you 'see' inside your head. It isn't simple and it isn't direct.

What I'm trying to say is: your brain creates your world. Everything exists inside your head.

The eye is the simple optical instrument that conveys this information. The brain is the engine of understanding but is less understood and more mysterious than the most distant star.

He gestures to the stars projected above.

Now, let's go back to the stars.

Ah, no stars.

Sorry everyone.

Can we have the projections now, please?

Projector please.

16. Total Darkness. Sound of the Crowd

Total Darkness. Sound.

The strangely voiceless sound of a hundred people rushing down steps past **Max***, who is negotiating the last few stairs of a short flight. In the near distance the unmistakable grind of escalators which sound as inviting as a giant mincing machine. Only a short stretch take us to the platform where the static hum of a train awaits.* **Max***'s stick more urgent as he tries to find a door. Sound of beeping as door closes leaving us hearing* **Max***'s POV of train disappearing into distance echoing down the tunnel. Litter blows in the draught created by the train.*

Fade.

17. The Packed Lunch Test

Home. Kitchen. SFX: Loud music, 'Green Onions' by Booker T and the MGs. **Max** *blindfolds himself and then practises getting* **Leo***'s packed lunch together for school.*

He fetches peanut butter, sliced bread and a knife and a lunchbox marked 'Leo'. He makes the sandwich, spreading the butter and carefully aligning the two slices of bread.

He fetches foil, crisps, an apple and a fizzy drink from a selection of cans in the fridge. He has chosen Heineken, which he places on the worktop while wrapping the sandwich in the foil. He puts the sandwich, drink, crisps and apple in the lunchbox. Mission complete, he removes the blindfold and checks his accomplishment by opening the lunchbox. He sees the Heineken, and consoles himself with a decent swig.

18. Recording Booth

Max *is sitting at the recording booth desk.*

Max   This is the constellation of Orion – after the Plough probably the most famous constellation in the night sky. If you take the left corner of his belt and extend down you come to Sirius –

Sorry.

Do you mind if I – Could I get a little bit more light in here – It's, it's quite difficult, sorry with the screen and erm . . . There's not a lot of . . . (I don't know . . . Just . . .)

. . . seeing what I need to in here . . .

Yeah.

OK.

Thank you, thank you.

This is the constellation of Orion – after the Plough probably the most famous constellation in the night sky. If you take the left corner of his belt and extend down you come to

Sirius, the brightest star in the sky: the Dog Star. For many
people Sirius is the first star they locate in the night sky.
There are two planets which are always brighter than Sirius,
Venus and Jupiter, but neither twinkles like Sirius. Twinkling
or distillation/*scintillation*! occurs when turbulence . . .

OK.

You want me to do it again.

No, no, I know this stuff backwards!

It's not that. It's just . . .

He sighs.

Just from the two planets.

OK.

There are two planets which are always brighter than Sirius,
Venus and Jupiter, but neither twinkles like Sirius. Twinkling
or *scintillation* occurs when turbulence in the Earth's
atmosphere causes the light coming to us from a star to
deviate, so the mostly white, slightly blue, of Sirius gets
broken down into many differing hues. Only Sirius is bright
enough to display these many brilliant colours to the naked
eye . . . And it was the first star I fell for.

Right.

You don't need me to do anything again?

You're sure?

OK.

No, I don't need any help. I can find my own way out. No, I
won't get lost.

19. Replaced in the Planetarium

Max *enters the planetarium alone. He looks up at where he could
once see the stars. The voiceover narration – which is not his, but
that of another voiceover artist and which is going to replace him –
begins as the music starts to play.*

Max   Fucking Vangelis!?

Voiceover Artist   This is the constellation of Orion – after the Plough probably the most famous constellation in the night sky. If you take the left corner of his belt and extend down you come to Sirius, the brightest star in the sky: the Dog Star.

For many people Sirius is the first star they locate in the night sky.

Max   For many people, for many people, for many people . . .

Voiceover Artist   There are two planets which are always brighter than Sirius, Venus and Jupiter, but neither twinkles like Sirius.

Twinkling or *scintillation* occurs when turbulence occurs in the earth's atmosphere and causes the light coming to us from a star to deviate, so the mostly white, slightly blue, of Sirius gets broken down into many differing hues.

Only Sirius is bright enough to display these many brilliant colours to the naked eye.

Max   And it was the first star I fell for . . .!

Fuck!

He cuts the music and playback dead with the remote control.

20. The Dream

Max   I dreamt I was in a great empty void, and I am gradually approaching an object – it's a box, a big ornate box, covered in an intricate pattern, a bit like the willow pattern – pale blue on white. The box has a huge presence, it's a big thing ominously sitting there in the middle of space. I'm being drawn towards it. As I get closer to it, a darkness appears on the top of it. The top starts to fold in on itself creating a kind of funnel, the pattern curves and stretches as the top bends into the centre. And so I fall or I am drawn into this aperture and I can see this distorted willow pattern as I pass through.

I am inside now and I gradually come down. As I descend I see a curtain or a drape. It has the same pattern as the outside of the box. I am looking down on a wide room with this huge curtain rising from the floor, all across the back wall. The room is empty except, in the foreground, there is a throne, and there is a man sitting on the throne. But everything is in miniature – it's a model set for a theatre; the throne is a little miniature throne with a tiny king with this big drape behind him.

And there is a feeling. A feeling of great sadness. The curtain begins to fall, slowly, and as it falls it makes a kind of music, the music is part of the falling – it's a note sung in a woman's voice – beautiful and overwhelmed with sadness and it's somehow bound up with this lonely little king. The drape finally falls and then there is this great terrible sob, this woman lets out this heavy sob from deep inside. I wake up.

21. In the Dark Room – Changing Faces

Max *is in his dark room. Music is playing in the sitting room next door. As* **Max** *develops another photograph we see that he is finding it even more difficult to read the labels on the chemical bottles. He is less sure of what he is doing, he strains to see the image on the photographic paper as it devolps in the tray. It is a picture of a face. As it develops it appears to melt, becoming horrifically distorted.* **Max** *recoils.*

22. Total Darkness. Sound of the Street

Total Darkness. Sound.

A quieter street than before: **Max**'s *tapping stick, the sound of rain and the occasional car passes, splashing water. We move past dripping foliage and an overflowing gutter. As he rounds a corner*

we hear a dual carriageway in the distance. The stick pauses. **Max**
*is not where he thought he was. He carries on, the traffic gets louder
and louder and louder.* **Max** *is confronted by a terrifying wall of
traffic. More unnervingly, he loses his sense of direction as the sound
of the traffic seems to be coming from all sides.*

Cut.

23. Shaving with Hallucinations

Leo We're going to make a rocket /

Max What? Right now?

Leo YES! /

Max OK!

Leo . . . and now I'm going to do a demonstration on the
other side – (*pehcew!*)

Max OK OK, but I need you to get ready, cos Grandad's
going to be here soon to babysit for you! So get your toys
together . . .

Thunderbirds Toy (*Geoff*) EVERY SECOND COUNTS!

Max Leo, please put Thunderbirds away, now.

Thunderbirds Toy (*Brains*) MR TRACY – DETONATION
IN FOUR SECONDS!

Max (*giving in a bit and joining in*) OK, BRAINS(?),
Thunderbirds are go!

Thunderbirds Toy (*Alan*) STAND BY FOR BLASTOFF!

Max Standing by!

Leo OK, we're gonna blast off, I think.

Max OK BLASTING OFF.

SFX: Thunderbirds Toys and **Max** *making noise and gestures to
leave planet Earth.*

Leo   Base control are you there?

Max (*taking on protocol voice*)   Roger. Base control here.
How're things up there? Over.

Leo   Mayday, mayday.

Max   What is it? Over!

Leo   We're going to steer into the moon.

Max   The moon, Leo???

Leo   And we're gonna take off part two when we've gone
past Saturn.

Max   Er, Saturn? What about the moon? Are you going to
the moon, OVER?

Leo   Yes, when we get past Jupiter.

Max   Jupiter? Are you a bit off course? Over?

Leo   OK we can see the very edge of Jupiter.

Max   Jupiter must have moved. Can you see Saturn?!

Leo   Saturn is very near, we need to avoid the asteroid
belt . . .

Max   Right take care up there – Over.

Leo   Right – we are landing on the moon!

Blast noises.

Max   You're on the moon? What's it look like? Over.

Leo   Our moon –

Max   It's one small step for a boy, one giant leap for
mankind. Over.

Leo   Our moon – I don't want to listen to you –

Max   Roger that, I suppose.

Leo   Oopsie I forgot this.

Max   What? Your space suit? Over?

Leo   OK, I've got it.

Max   OK. Ready for the moon walk?

Leo   I am doing the space walk now.

Max   Any aliens? Over?

Leo (*screams*)

Max   Are you OK? Over? Are there aliens? Over?

Leo   Mayday!

Max   What? Is there / . . .?

Leo   Warn the whole world that there's gonna be loads of rain.

Max   Lots of rain? Bad weather?

Leo   Base control did you read? Over.

Max   Roger – copy that. Bad rain on its way. Will send out global rain warning.

Max *looks back at the miror and starts to hallucinate.*

SFX reflects subjective panic mood of **Max**. *Music? Sound? as* **Max** *notices something in the shaving mirror and he is puzzled and perturbed by it – but transfixed while* **Leo** *continues reports in background.*

Leo   Um, we found something very mysterious . . .

Max *carries on transfixed in the mirror.*

Leo   . . . I'm gonna put this thing down and I found something but I don't know what it is, OK.

Max (*shouts, freaking out at the swooping birds*)   Get off me! Get off me! Shit!

Leo   Mayday! MAYDAY!

Max   Get off!

Leo   I ignore you!

Max (*very troubled*)   Leo, stop. Stop!

Leo   No. Mayday.

Max   Leo. Stop. Stop.

Leo   I ignore you, over!

Max   Leo! Stop! Game over!

Leo   I ignore you.

Max *stares at* **Leo**.

Leo   Daddy!

Max   Come here, Leo.

Leo   Stop staring at me, Daddy. /

Max   Leo . . . /

Leo   Stop it Dad. Stop staring at me Daddy.

Leo *runs out of sight, hiding in the room out of* **Max**'s *sight*.

Max   Leo! Leo! Come back!

He frantically looks around.

Max   Leo. Where are you?

Leo (*Thunderbirds blastoff sound*)

Max   Come out. I can't see you.

Leo's Toy (*Alan's voice*)   STAND BY FOR BLASTOFF!
(*SFX: rocket blast.*)

Max   Leo.

Thunderbirds Toy (*Virgil's voice*)   EVERY SECOND
COUNTS!

Max   Leo, stop it. Where are you?

Thunderbirds Toy (*Brains*)   MR TRACY – DETONATION
IN FOUR SECONDS!

Max Leo!

Thunderbirds Toy (*Penelope*)   PARKER, WE'RE
RUNNING OUT OF TIME.

Max Come here! Come HERE!

Thunderbirds Toy (*Brains*)   THAT WOULD BE VERY
RISKY MR TRACY.

Max Come here where I can see you!

His mobile phone starts ringing on his desk.

Max Leo! Where are you? Where are you?

SFX: Sound of a door opening, slamming.

Leo, stay here!

Leo!!

He answers the phone at last.

Yes?

What is it Dad?

Yes. What is it!?

I've got to go. I'll see you in a minute!!

Cuts him off.

Max OK. Leo! – Grandad's on his way. Please come out.
I'm sorry I shouted . . .

Leo's Thunderbird Toy   F.A.B. VIRGIL . . .

Max LEO!!

24. Planetarium with Hallucinations

Max 'How do we know where we are in the Universe?'
That's a good question.

Once we imagined that the Earth stood fixed at the centre of
a moving universe with the Sun, moon and all the stars and
planets turning about us . . .

Now we know that we're all moving at about 650 miles an hour as the Earth rotates on its axis. The Earth is going round the Sun at 43,000 miles an hour. The Milky Way galaxy is spinning like an enormous pinwheel with the Sun hurtling alongside billions of other stars at 483,000 miles per hour. And the entire Milky Way galaxy itself, as it spins, is travelling across space at a staggering 1.3 million miles per hour.

How can you be certain about anything you see from here on Earth, peering out into the darkness? How can you really know where you are in the universe?

There is no fixed point.

No fixed point in a universe that is getting bigger and bigger, rushing away from itself so fast that one day its light will never reach us.

The universe itself is going blind – going dark. Even when you look up, you are only seeing a fraction of this fading picture.

The more we find out about the cosmos the more we realise what we don't see, what we can't see, and what we will never see.

It's not so much about what your eyes can do, but what you can piece together in your mind, what you can feel, what you can perceive. Light and sight are not enough. You need to imagine the universe and to question it –

And when there is no fixed point – you have to choose one.

(*He halts in his tracks looking ahead of him.*) You have to choose one. (*Troubled.*) Sorry. (*He looks suddenly in a different direction.*) Sorry – And this question – I'm really sorry. Can you see . . .? (*He looks and focuses at several points in the room as if checking his vision.*) It's happening again.

(*He waves his hands and arms in front of his face as if trying fend off the swooping birds he is seeing.*) Excuse me one moment. I need to stop the show here. I'm sorry I need to stop the show. I need to get out.

25. Talking to Dad

Max *on mobile in corridor outside planetarium.*

Max (*flustered*)   Dad – I'm leaving work early.

I just walked out of the Q&A /

More hallucinations.

I saw a flock of birds swooping towards me – I thought they were going to hit me.

It's getting much more intense.

I keep trying to tell myself I'm not going nuts, but it feels like I am. This is really tough, Dad . . .

How's Leo? Is he alright?

Why was he crying? What did you say to him?

OK, OK, sorry. What did he say to you?

That's Dhruv. Why was he talking about that?

He asked if I'd forget him? Because of my sight?

He thinks I'll forget him because I can't see him.

Pause.

Dad, I need to talk to him. I need to talk to him now. I've got to get home.

No, I'll find my own way back. I'll find my own way home.

Bye.

26. Total darkness. The Sound of rain

Total darkness. Sound.

The sound of dual carriageway now quite distant and giving way to the sound of dripping from foliage. We hear the rumble receding further to give way to bird song, heard for the first time since the opening; the familiar suburban sound of a blackbird's alarm call.

Finally the stick slows. Grit under Max's heel as he turns slightly. A pause as all the distant traffic sounds we take for granted fade to silence save the microscopic sound of a drip coming from some leaves. We hear the sound of a metal garden gate swing open.

27. Max and Leo and Dhruv

Max *is standing in front of the Dhruv star mobile, lit, next to* **Leo's** *bed.*

The rain taps at the window. A long pause, as **Max** *sits and looks at* **Leo** . . . *runs into the next scene.*

28. What is it like to go blind . . . ?

Leo   Um, what is it like going blind? Is it blurry or is it like I'm a long long way from you?

Max   It's not blurry. It's not blurry . . .

Leo   Will you still be able to see me?

Max   No, Leo, I won't be able to see you . . .

Leo   I will still see you unless I go blind . . .

Max   You're not going to go blind. You'll still be able to see me.

Leo   But you won't be able to see me.

Long pause.

Leo   Will you see the stars at night?

Max   No, I really can't see the stars. You can though.

Leo   Can you see the Milky Way?

Max   No I can't see the Milky Way, can you?

Leo   Um, yes.

Max   I can see the non-star Milky Way, though.

Leo   Is there anything, if it was really black and you couldn't see a thing, would you be able, and there wasn't any light but it was a museum, would you be able to see any, if there was a mirror and that was shooting off light towards you, would you be able to see the light?

Max   I don't think so, but with all that help I'd certainly try my best!

Leo   If there was a really black night, I think it might be easier for you to see the bigger stars.

Max   Like Sirius?

Leo   Sirius is about that big . . . If I was going blind probably I'd be able to see the moon . . . and . . . it would almost be hard for me . . .

Max   It would be.

Leo   . . . To understand . . . I don't know . . . To understand how . . .

Max   It's hard to understand . . .

Leo   . . . How (*unintelligible*)

Max   Do you think it's hard for Daddy?

Leo   It would be more difficult to explain . . .

Max   Yes Leo, it is hard to explain. My eyes are playing tricks on me and I've been seeing things that aren't there. But whatever happens to my eyes, Leo, I will always know you're there.

Leo   How would you remember what I would look like with going blind?

Max   I'll never forget what you look like, Leo.

Leo   In your life?

Max   No, Leo, of course not.

Leo   But the brain gets confused with . . .

Max   Well I might get confused. But then I'll hear your voice and I'll know . . .

Leo   Can you still cry if you go blind?

Max   Do you think I'll be sad? Is that why you're asking me that?

Leo   Yes.

Max   Leo, we're going to be alright. We're going to be alright.

Pause.

Leo   This man may look like an idiot, he may sound like an idiot, but don't let that fool you: he really is an idiot.

Max *laughs.*

Max   You wee rascal, you.

Leo   Can I have a little test of feeling what it would be like being blind?

Max   Yeah? You want to do that?

Leo   Yeah.

Max   Oh OK! Have you got the glasses?

Leo   Um yeah!

Max   Can you put them on . . .?

Leo   Yes.

29. Into the Garden

Max   Hold my hand, Leo . . .

They go into the garden, into the rain.

Music. The sounds of rain, each forming its own layer. Another layer; **Leo***'s voice fading into the distance describing what he sees as* **Max***, close by and with beautiful clarity, tells us what he sees when he listens to the rain.*

If I listen carefully I can almost reach the far side of the garden.

The rain illuminates everything.

The silver birch tree.

Sound.

The concrete path. (*Sound.*) The grass. (*Sound.*) The pond The roof above . . . Our garden.

FX: everything floods into the sound.

And you.

The sound changes, the rain stops; the sound of an owl. Distant thunder. Lightning.

End.

Methuen Drama Modern Plays

include work by

Edward Albee
Jean Anouilh
John Arden
Margaretta D'Arcy
Peter Barnes
Sebastian Barry
Brendan Behan
Dermot Bolger
Edward Bond
Bertolt Brecht
Howard Brenton
Anthony Burgess
Simon Burke
Jim Cartwright
Caryl Churchill
Complicite
Noël Coward
Lucinda Coxon
Sarah Daniels
Nick Darke
Nick Dear
Shelagh Delaney
David Edgar
David Eldridge
Dario Fo
Michael Frayn
John Godber
Paul Godfrey
David Greig
John Guare
Peter Handke
David Harrower
Jonathan Harvey
Iain Heggie
Declan Hughes
Terry Johnson
Sarah Kane
Charlotte Keatley
Barrie Keeffe

Howard Korder
Robert Lepage
Doug Lucie
Martin McDonagh
John McGrath
Terrence McNally
David Mamet
Patrick Marber
Arthur Miller
Mtwa, Ngema & Simon
Tom Murphy
Phyllis Nagy
Peter Nichols
Sean O'Brien
Joseph O'Connor
Joe Orton
Louise Page
Joe Penhall
Luigi Pirandello
Stephen Poliakoff
Franca Rame
Mark Ravenhill
Philip Ridley
Reginald Rose
Willy Russell
Jean-Paul Sartre
Sam Shepard
Wole Soyinka
Simon Stephens
Shelagh Stephenson
Peter Straughan
C. P. Taylor
Theatre Workshop
Sue Townsend
Judy Upton
Timberlake Wertenbaker
Roy Williams
Snoo Wilson
Victoria Wood

Methuen Drama Contemporary Dramatists
include

John Arden (two volumes)
Arden & D'Arcy
Peter Barnes (three volumes)
Sebastian Barry
Dermot Bolger
Edward Bond (eight volumes)
Howard Brenton
  (two volumes)
Richard Cameron
Jim Cartwright
Caryl Churchill (two volumes)
Sarah Daniels (two volumes)
Nick Darke
David Edgar (three volumes)
David Eldridge
Ben Elton
Dario Fo (two volumes)
Michael Frayn (three volumes)
David Greig
John Godber (four volumes)
Paul Godfrey
John Guare
Lee Hall (two volumes)
Peter Handke
Jonathan Harvey
  (two volumes)
Declan Hughes
Terry Johnson (three volumes)
Sarah Kane
Barrie Keeffe
Bernard-Marie Koltès
  (two volumes)
Franz Xaver Kroetz
David Lan
Bryony Lavery
Deborah Levy
Doug Lucie

David Mamet (four volumes)
Martin McDonagh
Duncan McLean
Anthony Minghella
  (two volumes)
Tom Murphy (six volumes)
Phyllis Nagy
Anthony Neilsen (two volumes)
Philip Osment
Gary Owen
Louise Page
Stewart Parker (two volumes)
Joe Penhall (two volumes)
Stephen Poliakoff
  (three volumes)
David Rabe (two volumes)
Mark Ravenhill (two volumes)
Christina Reid
Philip Ridley
Willy Russell
Eric-Emmanuel Schmitt
Ntozake Shange
Sam Shepard (two volumes)
Wole Soyinka (two volumes)
Simon Stephens (two volumes)
Shelagh Stephenson
David Storey (three volumes)
Sue Townsend
Judy Upton
Michel Vinaver
  (two volumes)
Arnold Wesker (two volumes)
Michael Wilcox
Roy Williams (three volumes)
Snoo Wilson (two volumes)
David Wood (two volumes)
Victoria Wood

Methuen Drama Modern Classics

Jean Anouilh *Antigone* • Brendan Behan *The Hostage* • Robert Bolt *A Man for All Seasons* • Edward Bond *Saved* • Bertolt Brecht *The Caucasian Chalk Circle* • *Fear and Misery in the Third Reich* • *The Good Person of Szechwan* • *Life of Galileo* • *The Messingkauf Dialogues* • *Mother Courage and Her Children* • *Mr Puntila and His Man Matti* • *The Resistible Rise of Arturo Ui* • *Rise and Fall of the City of Mahagonny* • *The Threepenny Opera* • Jim Cartwright *Road* • *Two & Bed* • Caryl Churchill *Serious Money* • *Top Girls* • Noël Coward *Blithe Spirit* • *Hay Fever* • *Present Laughter* • *Private Lives* • *The Vortex* • Shelagh Delaney *A Taste of Honey* • Dario Fo *Accidental Death of an Anarchist* • Michael Frayn *Copenhagen* • Lorraine Hansberry *A Raisin in the Sun* • Jonathan Harvey *Beautiful Thing* • David Mamet *Glengarry Glen Ross* • *Oleanna* • *Speed-the-Plow* • Patrick Marber *Closer* • *Dealer's Choice* • Arthur Miller *Broken Glass* • Percy Mtwa, Mbongeni Ngema, Barney Simon *Woza Albert!* • Joe Orton *Entertaining Mr Sloane* • *Loot* • *What the Butler Saw* • Mark Ravenhill *Shopping and F***ing* • Willy Russell *Blood Brothers* • *Educating Rita* • *Stags and Hens* • *Our Day Out* • Jean-Paul Sartre *Crime Passionnel* • Wole Soyinka • *Death and the King's Horseman* • Theatre Workshop *Oh, What a Lovely War* • Frank Wedekind • *Spring Awakening* • Timberlake Wertenbaker *Our Country's Good*

Methuen Drama Student Editions

Jean Anouilh *Antigone* • John Arden *Serjeant Musgrave's Dance*
Alan Ayckbourn *Confusions* • Aphra Behn *The Rover* • Edward Bond
Lear • *Saved* • Bertolt Brecht *The Caucasian Chalk Circle* • *Fear and
Misery in the Third Reich* • *The Good Person of Szechwan* • *Life of Galileo* •
Mother Courage and her Children • *The Resistible Rise of Arturo Ui* • *The
Threepenny Opera* • Anton Chekhov *The Cherry Orchard* • *The Seagull* •
Three Sisters • *Uncle Vanya* • Caryl Churchill *Serious Money* • *Top Girls*
• Shelagh Delaney *A Taste of Honey* • Euripides *Elektra* • *Medea*•
Dario Fo *Accidental Death of an Anarchist* • Michael Frayn *Copenhagen*
• John Galsworthy *Strife* • Nikolai Gogol *The Government Inspector* •
Robert Holman *Across Oka* • Henrik Ibsen *A Doll's House* • *Ghosts*•
Hedda Gabler • Charlotte Keatley *My Mother Said I Never Should* •
Bernard Kops *Dreams of Anne Frank* • Federico García Lorca *Blood
Wedding* • *Doña Rosita the Spinster* (bilingual edition) •*The House of
Bernarda Alba* • (bilingual edition) • *Yerma* (bilingual edition) • David
Mamet *Glengarry Glen Ross* • *Oleanna* • Patrick Marber *Closer* • John
Marston *Malcontent* • Martin McDonagh *The Lieutenant of Inishmore* •
Joe Orton *Loot* • Luigi Pirandello *Six Characters in Search of an Author*
• Mark Ravenhill *Shopping and F***ing* • Willy Russell *Blood Brothers*
• *Educating Rita* • Sophocles *Antigone* • *Oedipus the King* • Wole
Soyinka *Death and the King's Horseman* • Shelagh Stephenson *The
Memory of Water* • August Strindberg *Miss Julie* • J. M. Synge *The
Playboy of the Western World* • Theatre Workshop *Oh What a Lovely
War* Timberlake Wertenbaker *Our Country's Good* • Arnold Wesker
The Merchant • Oscar Wilde *The Importance of Being Earnest* •
Tennessee Williams *A Streetcar Named Desire* • *The Glass Menagerie*

For a complete catalogue
of Methuen Drama titles
write to:

Methuen Drama
Bloomsbury Publishing Plc
50 Bedford Square
London WC1B 3DP

or you can visit our website at:

www.methuendrama.com